THE DRAGON EMPEROR

A
CHINESE
FOLKTALE

RETOLD BY WANG PING
ILLUSTRATIONS BY TANG GE

Ⅿ Millbrook Press/Minneapolis

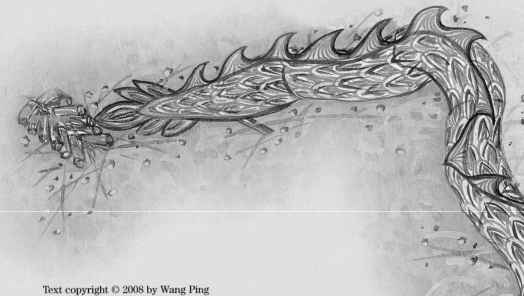

Millbrook Press
A division of Lerner Publishing Group, Inc.
241 First Avenue North
Minneapolis, MN 55401

Website address: www.lernerbooks.com

Library of Congress Cataloging-in-Publication Data

Wang, Ping.
    The dragon emperor / Retold by Wang Ping ; Illustrations by Tang Ge.
       p.   cm. — (On my own folkore)
    ISBN 978–0–8225–6740–0 (lib. bdg. : alk. paper)
    1. Folklore—China. I. Tang, Ge, ill. II. Title.
  PZ10.841.W295 2008
  398.2'0951—dc22   2006036718

Manufactured in the United States of America
1 2 3 4 5 6 – DP – 13 12 11 10 09 08

to Ariel and Leo
—W. P.

The Yellow Emperor

In the center of China stands Mount Tai.
Five-colored clouds
wrap around the mountain,
and rivers of yellow, red, black,
blue, and white flow down its sides.
Magical animals fill the thick forests
that cover the mountain's slopes.
Fantastic birds fly over the trees,
and fish swim in the streams.

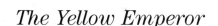

Mount Tai is also home
to gods and goddesses.
They have the faces of humans
and the bodies of snakes
with tails coiling
all the way up to their heads.
They eat the black-and-white jade
that is found on the mountain.

One night on Mount Tai, long ago,
a mother gave birth to a golden dragon.
He had four faces—
one on the front and one on the back,
one on the left and one on the right.
The baby was the Yellow Emperor.
He started talking in just a few days
and grew up quickly.
The Yellow Emperor became
a great leader in the region.

The Yellow Emperor
was more than just a ruler.
He was also an inventor.
He taught his people
how to use fire to cook raw food.
He invented the wok
to make cooking easier.

He also taught people where to dig wells
and how to build houses.
With cooked food,
clean water,
and safe homes,
his people grew stronger
and healthier.

The emperor supported his officials
as they created their own inventions.
Under his leadership, people studied
the sun, the moon, and the stars.

They invented written language
and Chinese characters.
They used this invention
to write down laws
and to create a calendar.
They recorded history and medicine.
They wrote about science and art.
Life in the Yellow Emperor's kingdom was good.

But peace was often broken
when neighboring tribes attacked.
The Yellow Emperor had to fight
to defend his land and people.
To help him battle his enemies,
he gathered clouds and rain.
He called upon the birds
and the animals to join him.

The Yellow Emperor also created inventions
to help his soldiers fight.
He invented war chariots
so that his army could move faster.
He created battle banners
so that his soldiers
could follow their commanders' orders
from far and near.

The Black Dragon

One of the Yellow Emperor's greatest
warriors was the Black Dragon,
named Chi You.
He drove the Yellow Emperor's chariot
and served as a top minister in his court.
He was also the leader
of nine powerful tribes in the land.
Chi You had four eyes
on his horned, steel head,
and six arms on his scaly body.
He could summon winds and rains.
He used these powers in battle
to destroy his enemies.

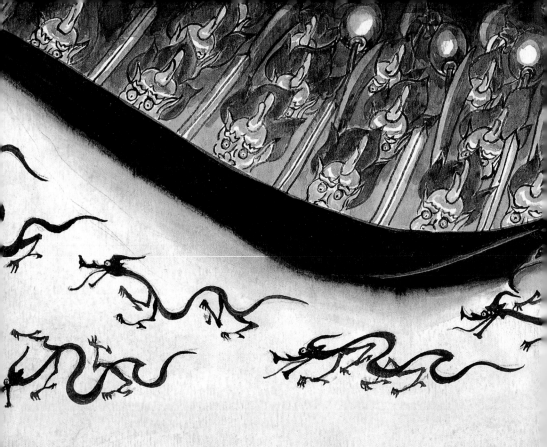

Chi You had 81 brothers
who were all just like him.
They were giant warriors
who ran like horses
and flew like birds.

They ate sand, rocks,
and metal for meals.
Chi You and his brothers
were the fiercest fighters
in the land.

But as his power and fame grew,
Chi You was no longer happy
with his position in the emperor's court.
He wanted to be emperor himself.
So he gathered his 81 brothers
and attacked the Yellow Emperor.

The Yellow Emperor and his army
met them outside the capital.
A long, fierce war began.

Dragons, tigers, lions, and bears
joined the Yellow Emperor's army.
Phoenixes, eagles, and hawks
flew over the battlefields,
forming flags to lead the army's way.
Gods from the mountains and rivers
rushed forward to help the Yellow Emperor
defend his country.

Chi You's army included
his 81 dragon brothers
and thousands of monster warriors.
He armed his soldiers
with swords, spears, and axes.
He gave them bows and arrows.
These were the newest
and most powerful weapons of the time.

Chi You was not only a great warrior.
He was also a mighty wizard.
He could cast spells on his enemies,
making them lose their minds
and their will to fight.

He could scare the wits
out of enemy soldiers
with mysterious mists
and strange noises.

During one battle, Chi You sent a thick fog
over the Yellow Emperor's battleground.
The emperor's army got lost in the mist.
Chi You's warriors
charged into the camp.
They killed so many soldiers
that blood formed a thick river.

The Yellow Emperor
and his remaining soldiers
wandered three days and nights
without water or food.
They were exhausted and confused,
on the edge of total defeat.

Then one of the emperor's inventors
built a special chariot.
It held the figure of a man
pointing his finger.
No matter which direction
the chariot turned,
the finger always pointed south.

The driver could never be lost.
This invention was
the world's first compass.
With it, the Yellow Emperor
could move through the fog.
He broke Chi You's siege
and led his soldiers
safely back to camp.

Even so, Chi You won
the first nine battles of the war.
The Yellow Emperor knew that
he needed greater inventions
to fight Chi You's dark magic.
First, he made bugles
out of bull and sheep horns.
When Chi You made his strange,
frightening noises,
the emperor's soldiers blew the horns.
They made deep sounds,
like dragons' roars.

They gave the soldiers back their courage
so they could fight Chi You's army
with all their strength.

Then the Yellow Emperor
captured the Thunder Dragon Kui
in the East China Sea.
He used his skin and bones
to make 82 magic drums.
When his soldiers beat the drums,
the thunderous sounds
traveled thousands of *li* across the land.
The drumbeats rocked the earth
like an earthquake.

Chi You's soldiers fell to the ground.
As they shivered and scrambled for cover,
the Yellow Emperor's army
charged in full force.
With the magic drums
of the Thunder Dragon,
the Yellow Emperor won his first victory.

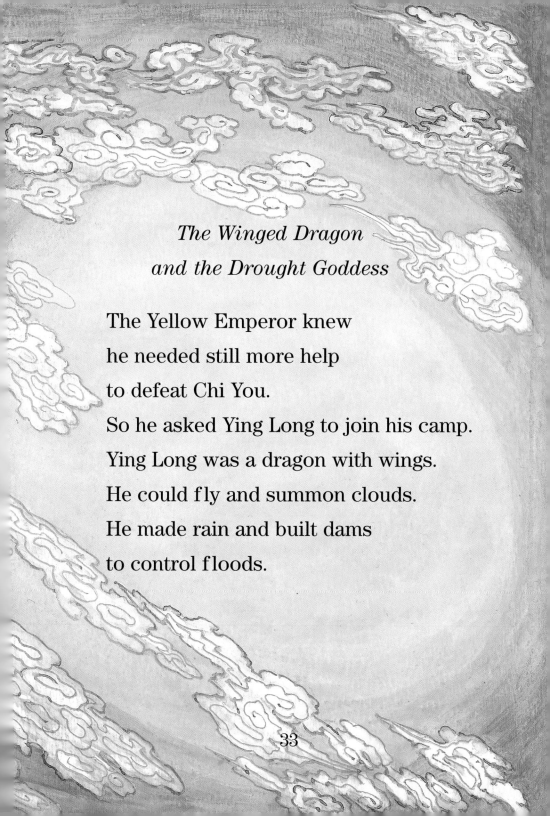

The Winged Dragon
and the Drought Goddess

The Yellow Emperor knew
he needed still more help
to defeat Chi You.
So he asked Ying Long to join his camp.
Ying Long was a dragon with wings.
He could fly and summon clouds.
He made rain and built dams
to control floods.

When the Yellow Emperor
asked him for help,
Ying Long built a dam.
He planned to fill a lake
behind the dam with water.
When he opened the dam,
the water would flood
Chi You's camp.

But Chi You moved quickly.
He summoned his own gods
of wind and rain.
He hurled a huge storm
upon the Yellow Emperor's camp
before the dam was finished.
Pouring rain flooded the battleground.
Many soldiers drowned.

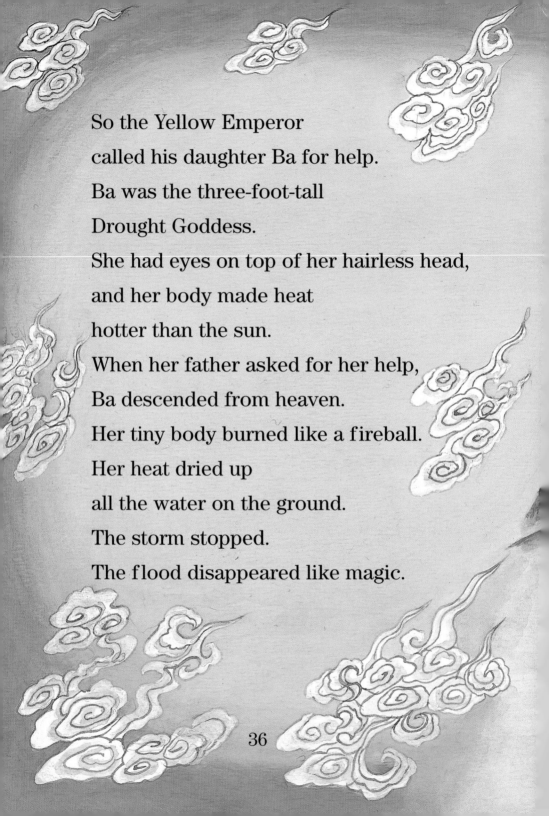

So the Yellow Emperor
called his daughter Ba for help.
Ba was the three-foot-tall
Drought Goddess.
She had eyes on top of her hairless head,
and her body made heat
hotter than the sun.
When her father asked for her help,
Ba descended from heaven.
Her tiny body burned like a fireball.
Her heat dried up
all the water on the ground.
The storm stopped.
The flood disappeared like magic.

Ying Long grabbed this chance
to finish his dam.
He filled the dam's lake with rain.
Then, opening the gates of the dam,
he flooded Chi You's camp.

He hurled more and more
storms and winds
at the Black Dragon's soldiers.
Before Chi You's army could recover,
the Yellow Emperor's army charged.
They captured the Black Dragon.
The Yellow Emperor ordered
that Chi You be killed.

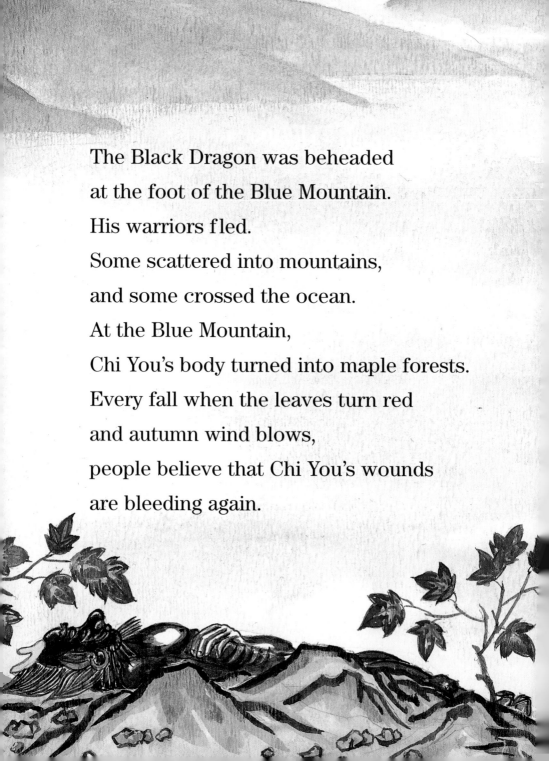

The Black Dragon was beheaded
at the foot of the Blue Mountain.
His warriors fled.
Some scattered into mountains,
and some crossed the ocean.
At the Blue Mountain,
Chi You's body turned into maple forests.
Every fall when the leaves turn red
and autumn wind blows,
people believe that Chi You's wounds
are bleeding again.

In the wind, they hear his spirit
calling his warrior brothers
for another rebellion.

Emperor of the Middle Kingdom

Defeating Chi You
made the Yellow Emperor
China's only ruler.
He reigned from Mount Tai.
With his four faces,
he watched over the world far and near.
He was called the Central Emperor,
and his country was called
zhong guo—the Middle Kingdom.

After the war, the Yellow Emperor
ordered his soldiers to gather together
all the spears and arrows and axes.
He told them to melt the weapons.
Then he had his best craftsmen
make a giant tripod from the melted metal.
Artists carved dragons and gods, beasts and
birds, plants and monsters on the tripod.
They showed scenes from the long battle.
They wanted people in the future
to remember what had happened.

At a great celebration
after the tripod was finished,
Ying Long appeared from the sky.
The golden scales on his wings and body
blinded the onlookers' eyes.
The winged dragon had returned to Earth
to take the Yellow Emperor
back to the heavenly court.
As everyone who watched
cried and begged him to stay,
the Yellow Emperor
stepped onto the dragon's back
and disappeared into the sky.

But the Yellow Emperor's spirit and wisdom
have lasted to this day.
He is remembered and worshipped
as China's number-one dragon.
And the people of China see themselves
as children of the Yellow Dragon.

Afterword

Dragons have been the most powerful creatures in Chinese folklore for thousands of years. In traditional tales, they are heavenly beings with deer's horns, camel's heads, ghost's eyes, snake's necks, and bull's ears. They have alligator's bellies, carp's scales, tiger's paws, and eagle's claws. In their mouths, they hold pearls that shine like stars. They can fly, swim, and dig great tunnels. Breathing fire and clouds, they move between the sky and the earth and the underworld.

Stories of these dragons are closely tied to Chinese emperors and China's creation. Rulers such as the Yellow Emperor often claimed that they were dragons. They appeared in human form but lived in dragon palaces, sat on dragon thrones, and wore dragon robes.

Dragons are still important to Chinese culture. The Yellow Emperor is seen as China's founder. And Chi You's descendants have never forgotten their leader's magic power. During festivals, they hold wrestling and martial arts competitions in his honor. At his temples, banners flutter loudly in the wind as if he were still making war cries. But Ying Long, the winged dragon, is the most popular dragon of all. On New Year's Day, people perform dragon dances for him. They hope to please him so that their new year will be blessed with rains, sunshine, and a great harvest.

Further Reading

The British Museum: Ancient China
  http://www.ancientchina.co.uk/
  This website from The British Museum introduces the crafts, geography, and history of ancient China.

Jango-Cohen, Judith. *Chinese New Year*. Minneapolis: Carolrhoda Books, Inc., 2005. Beautiful art and lively text introduce an important Chinese holiday.

Glossary

characters: symbols used in writing. The Chinese alphabet is made up of characters.

drought: a long period of dry weather

emperor: the ruler of a country

jade: a hard stone

li: a Chinese unit for measuring distance

phoenixes: imaginary birds that often appear in stories and myths

tripod: a bowl or pot with three legs

wok: a round pan used in Chinese cooking